Gypsy on 18 Wheels

Gypsy on 18 Wheels

A Trucker's Tale

Robert Krueger

Edited by Sam Yanes

Praeger Publishers
New York

Published in the United States of America in 1975
by Praeger Publishers, Inc.
111 Fourth Avenue, New York, N.Y. 10003

Library of Congress Cataloging in Publication Data
Yanes, Sam, 1946-
    Gypsy on 18 wheels; a trucker's tale.

    1. Yanes, Sam, 1946-   I. Krueger, Robert, joint
author. II. Title.
TL140.Y36A33   388.3′24′0924 [B]   74-2692
ISBN 0-275-51970-8
ISBN 0-275-63350-0 (pbk.)

Printed in the United States of America

Acknowledgments

Grateful acknowledgment is made for the use of the following material:

Songs:

Big Bertha, Truck Drivin' Queen ("I was ridin' my thumb out across the state"), by Bill Eldridge, Gary Stewart, and Glenn Shell; published by Forrest Hills Music, Inc., Nashville, Tennessee; distributed by BMI. *Big Wheel Cannon Ball (Wabash Cannonball)* ("This great and mighty nation will sing forever more"), by Vaughn Horton; published by Seven Music Publishing, Inc., New York, New York; distributed by ASCAP (also public domain). *Black Smoke Blowin' over 18 Wheels* ("Well, woman, don't you put no bets on me"), author unknown. *Caffein, Nicotine, Benzedrine, and Wish Me Luck* ("Been pushin' that diesel since early dawn"), by Bill Hayes, Bill Howard, and Betty Mackey; published by Forrest Hills Music, Inc., Nashville, Tennessee; distributed by BMI. *Diesel Smoke and Dangerous Curves* ("I'm drivin' a truck on a mountain road"), by Cal Martin; published by Johnstone-Montei, Inc., c/o Beechwood Music, Hollywood, California; distributed by BMI. *Truck Driver's Blues* ("Feelin' tired and weary from my head down to my shoes"), by Ted Daffan. *Forty Acres* ("He headed into Boston in a big long diesel truck"), by Randell Bennett and Robert Paul Bennett; distributed by BMI. Also by David Romain; published by Random Music Co., Chicago, Illinois; distributed by ASCAP. *Going Down the Road* ("I'm going down that road feelin' bad"), by Jack Hardy. *How Fast Them Trucks Will Go* ("You know, a lotta folks stop at truckstops"), author unknown. *I Fought with the Diesel and the Diesel Won* ("Some men were born to read the Gospel"), author unknown. *If the World Ran out of Diesel,* author unknown. *I'm a Truck* ("You've heard songs about truck drivers"), by Red Simpson. *Ravishing Ruby* ("Ravishing Ruby, she's been around for a while"), by Tom T. Hall; published by Hallnote Music, Nashville, Tennessee. *Semi Truck* ("Well, I haul my rig out of San Jose"), by Farlow and Kirchen; published by Famous Music

Corp., New York, New York; distributed by BMI. *Six Days on the Road* ("Well, I pulled out of Pittsburgh rollin' down that Eastern Seaboard"), by Earl Greene and Carl Montgomery; published by Newkeys Music, Inc., c/o Jimmy Key, Nashville, Tennessee; distributed by BMI. Also published by Tune Music, Inc., Florence, Alabama; distributed by BMI. *Speedball Tucker* ("I drive a broke-down rig on 'may-pop' tires"), by Jim Croce; published by Blendingwell Music, Inc., New York, New York. *Truck Driver's Queen* ("Ain't got time to play the pinball"), author unknown. *Truck Drivin' Man* ("I stopped at a roadhouse in Texas"), by Alan Fraser; published by Northern Comfort Publishing, Cookshire, Quebec, Canada; distributed by BMI. Also by Rickey Coonce; published by ABC Dunhill Music, Los Angeles, California; distributed by BMI. Also by Marten Brown; distributed by BMI. *The Truck Drivin' Man* ("Won't you shake hands, buddy, with a truck drivin' man"), by Bennie Hess; published by Grandwealth Music Co., Nashville, Tennessee; distributed by BMI. *Truck Drivin' Woman* ("She was a truck drivin' woman"), by Eddie Hazelwood and Tex Atchison; published by Ridgeway Music Co., Inc., Hollywood, California; distributed by BMI. Also by Walt Pascoe; published by Cal Pascoe Publishing, Bakersfield, California; distributed by BMI. Also by Murray Wecht, published by New York Times Music Corp., New York, New York; distributed by BMI. *A Trucker's Life* ("Every pretty girl that pa$ses me by"), author unknown. *White Line Fever (Working Man's Blues),* by Merle Haggard, published by Blue Book Music, Bakersfield, California; distributed by BMI.

Glossary:

Entries are taken from Montie Tak, *Truck Talk* (Philadelphia: Chilton Book Co., 1971).

Contents

Introduction

You know, a lotta folks stop at truck stops
they just naturally think they should
they think that any place a truck driver eats
The food's just bound to be good

So they go in there amongst them gear jammers
settin' round talkin' low
Talkin' about women and stuff like that
And how fast them trucks will go

Now there's a little ole place out on 66
Where a lotta the boys stop and get their kicks
reckless eyeballing that waitress they call Flo
There's a lotta the bunch there, hangin' out
cuttin' the fool and talkin' about
How she wiggles when she walks and stuff like that
and how fast them trucks will go

Well I can't explain how it makes you feel
but you tip her five bucks on a two-dollar meal
You grab your hat and start headin' out kinda slow
While you're pushin' your diesel on down the line
You get to thinkin' about the women you left behind
How she wiggles when she walks, and stuff like that
And how fast them trucks will go

Somewhere along the line we have come to believe that truck stops serve the best food on the road. Don't you believe it! Not wanting to fight a good old American tradition, we dutifully follow the trucker to the gastric slaughter of acid coffee and chicken-fried steak, but not to the familiar mom and pop truck stop. They're gone, replaced in the American way by the glass and aluminum surrogates erected by the large oil companies. But the truckers are there, so it must be all right.

Gone, too, is the booth in the back corner where a hairy hand would reach out periodically to paw a passing waitress, who was forever returning to fill empty coffee cups. The back booth has been replaced by the formica counter of the "truckers only" gearjammers' section of the company restaurants.

I'm sure I'm not the only one who has eyed the back booths and gearjammers' corners with a certain amount of wonder, envy (maybe their food was edible), and even awe. Pretty soon my curiosity got the best of me, and after a careful study of trucker etiquette I began traveling in levis, work shirts, and boots. I practiced mounting the counter stool in the traditional crotch-first attitude, and then sitting with my ass hanging at least a foot over the back of the stool. (This is probably because it is so tender from bouncing around for the last 200 miles down an Interstate. To "tourist traffic" that 200 miles is a smooth, gently swaying ride, but in a truck cab it's more like riding a buckboard full tilt over the ties of a railroad track.) I found that if I slouched enough it would cover the absence of a spare tire normally brought on by too many mealy hamburgers, soggy fries, doughy biscuits, too much imitation gravy and instant mashed potatoes, not enough sleep, and too many hours. The hemorrhoids, I thought, I could let pass. Keeping my ears open I could pick up enough slang so nobody could tell I was driving a VW rather than a KW.

This book is the result of more chicken-fried steaks and bad coffee than I care to think about, and more hours riding shotgun than my newly acquired hemorrhoids should be forced to count. This is not *about* but rather *by* a group of men and a few brave women who represent, more than any swivel-jockey, what the American dream is, or at best was, all about.

Now it seems to be the American dream gone sour. The truck shutdowns of the past few years affected most of us only to the extent that for a few days some of our groceries were a little hard to get. In the long run, though, this will be known as the beginning of the end of one of the last free-wheeling, "I'm my own boss" ways of life. These guys who represent the backbone of the silent majority are beginning to pick up on how larger business interests manipulate the economy. They know damn well that someone is making a bundle because they haul the goods, and that someone sure isn't them. They may not be up on the latest news; it's hard to read much and drive 150,000 to 300,000 miles a year. But they're questioning the philosophy of "What's good for GM is good for the country," because GM sure isn't helping to pay their bills.

All of a sudden, the independent free spirit of the trucker is caught in the Catch 22 of the squeeze between government regulations and bureaucracy on one hand, and the sheer burden of the cost of operation on the other. Already, many independent truckers have been forced to park their rigs and seek company jobs or get out of trucking altogether.

You might—and a majority of people probably do—have the idea that being a trucker is some sort of glamorous job, sitting around truck stops all day hustling waitresses. We did it to the cowboy. Who did you think was riding the range while all the ''boys'' were running into town to get drunk, make it with the barmaid, and clean up at the poker tables? Any realistic cowboy movie would be as long and as boring as the trucker's life, with long periods of boredom broken occasionally by a little diversion that gets blown out of proportion.

So to all these hairy-handed, out-of-shape, hospitable, generous, honest, lying truckers who wrote all this, I'd like to dedicate this book.

Keep it between the ditches.

Bob Krueger

Raton, New Mexico

The Romance of the Road

This great and mighty nation will sing forever more
Of the pioneers, brave engineers, and heroes by the score,
But the world of transportation has its own brand
    just as great,
It's the men of steel behind the wheel
Of the big rigs haulin' freight.

Listen to the rumble, listen to the roar
Of the big wheels on the highways
From the mountains to the shore.
Old Buffalo Bill and Casey Jones would never have the gall
To risk their fate on the Interstate
On the Big Wheel Cannon Ball.

I've watched a thousand sunsets through this windshield. This is sort of the last frontier, where a guy can roam, be his own boss, and not listen to a whole lot. I do everything myself. I do as I please. If I want to go someplace, I just catch a load going there. I mix my traveling with what I want to do. Oh, I suppose that there's more things that would be more gratifying in the pocketbook, but you get to see everything my way. You just can't do it in other professions. You're nailed down to one spot. Even drivin' for one of the big freight companies would be like factory work to me.

I can't remember ever not wanting to drive. I had my name engraved on this truck insignia for my twelfth birthday, and I can remember just lookin' at all the trucks go by, even though they were just cattle and grain haulers. In those days, most kids would stand along the railroad tracks and wave at the engineer. Now they stand along the highway. Kids love trucks. It's got some romance to it.

Some men were born to read the Gospel,
Some men were born to heal the sick,
But I was born to drive a big old diesel,
And buddy, let me tell you, ain't no small trick.

Some men were born to teach children,
Some men were born to read the law,
But I was born to drive a big old diesel,
A curse handed down to me by my Pa.

I been jammin' gears and wheelin' this diesel
Up and down every road in the land.
Sometimes it gets so tough, the road gets rough,
But I'm a natural-born truck drivin' man.

Some men were born to be great lovers,
Some men were born to carry a gun,
But I was born to drive a big old diesel.
I fought with the diesel and the diesel won.

TENN.______2117
ARK.___M-2981
KY.__________440
MISS.______6323
OHIO.__10008-1X
MICH.__L-12829
MO.P.S.C....T-18983
KANS. K.C.C....5583
OKLA....M.C.-22157
MINN........21453
COLO. P.U.C. 4638-1
IOWA.......44037
WIS.I.C......9655

A Ma-and-Pa truck stop, Little Lake, California

Union 76 truck stop, Oglala, Nebraska

There are guys that drive strictly 'cause it's a good payin' job. There's nothin' wrong with that. Then there's the guys— with them it's a way of life. Me, I just started. I was semi-working as a mechanic just hangin' around places until I got a job. I started out drivin' dump trucks haulin' grain and gravel. It's the only job an inexperienced driver can get. The big companies all want drivers with ten to fifteen years under their belts. See, when you start out, you're at the age when you want money. Then you get to the age when you want security. That's why a lot of experienced guys work for companies.

I'd never work for a big company. They'd always be tellin' me what to do. I just want my own truck, nothin' fancy. You know, I've quit three different times, but it's in my blood. I just keep comin' back to drivin'.

My truck's got 611,000 miles on it, and it's still real tight. You don't have to spend a lot of money on a truck, you just have to buy it at the right moment in its cycle. A freight company will buy a truck and keep it for about five years. When they get rid of it, a guy like me ends up with it. Then it lasts another fifteen years. Then it gets retired to haulin' grain or gravel. After that it's the bone pile.

Trucks are kinda like race cars. At Indianapolis, a lot of those cars have been around for ten years. The components keep changin'. It's kinda hard to describe, but it's your *equipment,* it's what you're used to, it's what you prefer. The guys get to feel strangely possessive about their trucks. The truck feels the same way. It gets used to one driver. If another guy starts drivin' and he shifts a little differently, the transmission doesn't like it. Oh, some are considered better than others, like Peterbilt, which they say is the Rolls Royce of trucks, but that is for when you are a kid and have illusions. As the illusions disappear, it doesn't really matter anymore 'cause each guy feels his truck is the best for him, and it is. There are only a few hand-built trucks left—Peterbilt, Kenworth, and Brockway. The mass-produced rigs have all those financing businesses built into the system. They make it easy for a guy to buy one very expensive truck, but a lot of guys just don't know how much it costs to haul. They get the truck, but don't have enough money invested to keep it going. It all catches up with you. It's the kind of business that you can take a lot out of right away, but when it comes time to put it back in, you might not have it. With truck payments alone running $700 a month, it can catch up with you, and you're outa business.

And yet, you ask any driver that's young and been drivin' for a few years what they want to do, and they'll say, "buy me a rig of my own.'' And he'll want one of the chrome-tanked ones. When you ask him why, he'll say, ''Boy, wouldn't you like to drive somethin' like that around!''

You've heard songs about truck drivers.
Many times their story's told.
How they rolled out of Pittsburgh for six days on the road,
'Bout the Feather River Canyon
And climbin' the old grapevine,
That old roadhouse down in Texas,
And the girls they've left behind.
You've heard their tales of daring
And I think that's just fine.
But if you can spare a minute
I'd like to tell you mine.

There'd be no truck drivers if it wasn't for us trucks.
No double clutchin', gear jammin', coffee drinkin' nuts.
They'll ride their way to glory
And they have all the luck.
There'd be no truck drivers if it wasn't for us trucks.

If we're on time he takes the credit,
If we're late I get the blame.
Up those hills with shutters open,
My stacks are runnin' flame.
My tack is runnin' red lines,
Suckin' diesel from the tanks.
I take him south and bring him back
Without a word of thanks.
So now you've heard my story and I guess its my tough luck.
There'd be no truck drivers if it wasn't for us trucks.

I taught this young guy how to drive a couple of weeks ago. He got the whole thing down in a week or so. Before that, he went down to check out one of those truck drivin' schools. He said they give about seventy hours of bookwork, studying regulations, how to make out logs, and how to read road maps. Reading road maps—can you imagine that?

He headed into Boston in a big long diesel truck.
His first trip to Boston, he was having lots of luck.
Goin' the wrong direction on a one way street in town,
And this is what he said when the police chased him down.
Give me forty acres and I'll turn this rig around.
It's the easiest way that I've found.
Some guys can turn it on a dime, or turn it right downtown,
But I need forty acres to turn this rig around.

When he finally found out where to unload, he had a
*   dreadful shock*
His trailer pointed to the road, his tractor to the dock
And as he looked around him through his tears he
*   made this sound*
Oh, give me forty acres and I'll turn this rig around.

With tears streamin' down his cheeks, they all heard him yell
Give me forty sticks of dynamite and I'll blow this rig to hell.

You can drive a truck longer and safer than a car. A trucker prepares himself mentally. It certainly isn't his physical conditioning that keeps him going. You'd be surprised by the number of heart attacks. Truckers don't eat properly, and a lot of 'em have hemorrhoids. I've had to get mine operated on quite a few times. I had to install "air-ride" seats in the truck. I think the hardest part of drivin' may be your bottom.

But you feel good up there in the cab. With more and more trucks on the road every day, you get so you just don't notice the passenger cars, except for good reason. I caught a glimpse of this girl coming from Cincinnati. I pulled along side of her car. She had her dress unbuttoned down to her belly button. All the other passenger cars could see were her shoulders. You get her up there with those big windows and those gals can't hide nothin'. 'Course maybe they don't want to.

Every pretty girl that passes me by,
I blow my horn and blink my lights.
Oh lord, what a life.
Up all day and up all night,
Drivin' this semi is what I like.
Oh lord, what a life.
One cup of coffee after another,
A few stolen moments with another man's lover.
Oh lord, what a life.
I'll get away from a naggin' wife,
Don't tell me this way ain't right.
Oh lord, what a life.
A trucker's life is the life for me.
On the road's where I've got to be.
I like it, yes sir-ey.
Oh lord, what a life.

Wichita's usually 'bout as far west as I go, and Wheeling's about as far east, which makes me happy 'cause I never want to go to New York again with their hijackings and Mercedes-Benz chrome garbage trucks. That's like going out to dinner at a truck stop with some classy broad with an evening gown on. I am gonna go to Denver for the National Truck Roadeo. I always have a pretty good time at that.

These roadeos are sponsored by the American Trucking Association, so they're directed more toward the trucking firms than the independents. You have to belong to a state association to participate, and the companies foot the bill for the guys and their families to come. I have a lot of mixed feelings about the thing. They claim it's primarily a safety event sponsored by a safety organization, but the primary concern is how to make money through safety. "A safe driver is an efficient driver," and so on.

ANNOUNCER FOR WWVA, WHEELING, WEST VIRGINIA, AT THE NATIONAL TRUCK ROADEO

"We have here Junior E. Reed riding for Timber Trucking Company in West Virginia. We'd like to congratulate you. You're twenty-three years of age. How long have you been drivin'?"

"Five years."

"What about your competition? This is the first time they've had 'flat-bed' contests. Is this pretty stiff?"

"They've had it for two years in West Virginia."

"What did you do last year?"

"Came in third."

"Already you've made it into the finals in the National Truck Driver Roadeo here. That makes it look like you did some practicing. Well, we're real proud of you due to the fact you're from West Virginia. Our station is, of course, from West Virginia, and we want to congratulate you and at the same time wish you good luck tomorrow. And by the way, how's the competition? Will it be extremely stiff?"

"No."

"You've got 200 other drivers to drive against. Did you watch any of the others yesterday?"

"You're not allowed to watch others in your class."

They get professional-conscious, and try to foster the image of the trucker as the gentleman of the highways, making our roads safe for the general public. It's sort of like the Boy Scouts. They have a rookie-of-the-year award in each of the thirty states holding a state association roadeo. They judge 'em on his attitude, community spirit, personality, safety record, and driving ability. Then they pick a National Roadeo rookie of the year on how they do in the competition. They even call the women who see that all the contestants are signed in and get to the events all right den mothers.

Last year, this safety inspector gave me a real hard time. She started telling me that all us fly-by-night gypsies are hurting the whole trucking industry, that real truckers were mature, upright professionals who didn't spit outa windows, chase after waitresses, and keep his equipment together with chewing gum.

I have fun, though, and the guys aren't anything like the organizers. I think it's a little embarrassing sometimes when they don't show the company-type enthusiasm that's expected.

For a while, we were losing our camaraderie on the road. It grew to such proportions that nobody'd stop and help anybody. Years ago, of course, everybody was real tight, but then nobody was makin' much money. Now these citizen-band radios are bringing us back together. We talk to each other, tell about scales, fuel, radar, and the like. Those things are real important. All we had before was the regular music radio stations. Stations like WWVA and WBAP. They'd give out road information on the air and pass on messages between songs. Most of the guys like Charlie Douglass down in New Orleans.

Those stations are geared to truckers, 'cause the truckers sort of took them under their wings. Made 'em a contact point for themselves and others. They like the music and the lyrics are down to earth. They recall a lot of situations we have in common. Listenin' to that rock stuff is worse than takin' speed. It jumps all over the cab just makin' everything nervous.

Some of the songs reflect an accurate picture of the truck driver and some don't. "Pour Me Another Cup of Coffee" is real popular, and of course all of Dave Dudley. The pills were at their peak in the late 'fifties and early 'sixties, when makin' good money meant stayin' awake. Now the guys that take pills are the guys who screw off. They stay an extra day in Denver and then have to make up the time.

One of my favorites is "I'm a Sailor On a Concrete Sea."

"But you heard about the others, right? I understand that they're pretty good."

"Oh, they're fair to middlin'."

"How in the world did we get so many West Virginians winning these events?"

"By chance."

"Think you mountain boys just have more training?"

"Running some of the awful roads in West Virginia should give us some experience."

"Well, we wish you the best of luck."

1973 National Truck Roadeo, Denver

The trucker has always had an image as a tough, self-made loner cutting himself off from the rest of society, and especially from women. (That is except when he feels the need for a little bit of "it.") It's hard to find an American hero who wasn't molded from the same stuff. A hundred years ago it was the cowboy, fifty years ago the hobo or railroad engineer, and today it's the truck driver. The theme of hard-working independence and responsible drifting is common to each of these heroic occupations. This similarity has not been lost on the writers and performers of country music, for whom the trucker has become the symbol of the twentieth-century hold-out for simple, yet hazardous, self-made satisfaction.

It pretty much all started in 1939 when Ted Daffan wrote the first trucking song, "Truck Drivin' Blues," and Humphrey Bogart and George Raft made the movie *They Drive By Night*. Daffan took two of the most universal themes in country music—honky-tonk women and whisky—and added the truck driver, which has become a successful format for country trucker songs.

Feelin' tired and weary from my head down to my shoes
Got a low-down feelin', truck driver's blues.
Keep them wheels a-rollin', I ain't got no time to lose
Got a low-down feelin', truck driver's blues.
I'm gonna ride, ride, ride on into town.
There's a honky-tonk gal a-waitin'
and I've got troubles to drown.
Never did have nothin', I got nothin' much to lose
Just a low-down feelin', truck driver's blues.

It wasn't until the 'sixties, in a song written by two Southern truckers, "Six Days on the Road," that this form began to transform the trucker into a full-blown country hero. Today there are a half-dozen or so country singers who do nothing else but trucker songs; over 300 have been written in the last fifteen years.

There are a number of country music radio stations around the country with all-night shows of standardized format geared to the trucker alone. Their range and spread are such that you could travel from coast to coast without missing a single song or equipment ad.

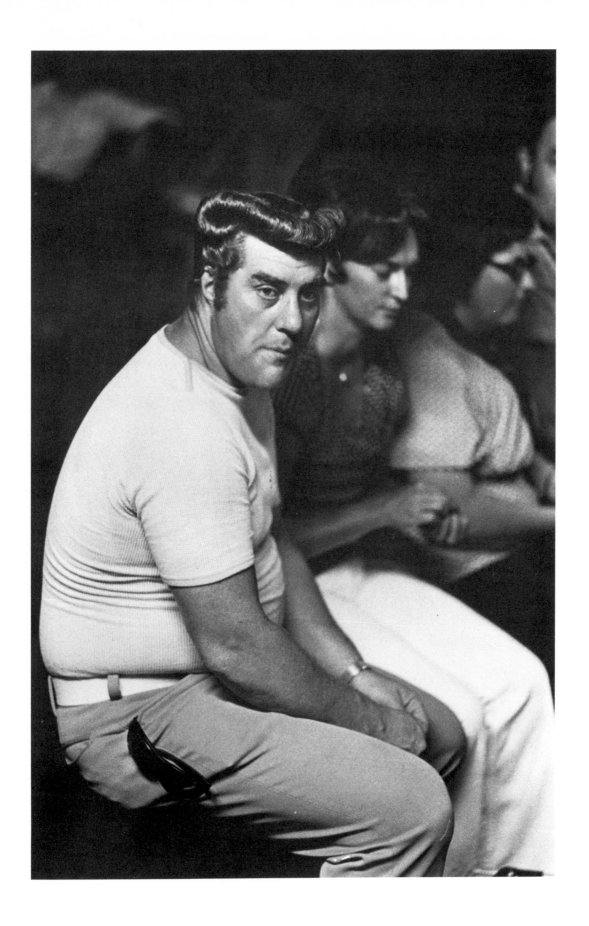

Dick Curles and fans, WWVA, Truckers' Jamboree

Dodge City, Kansas

Been pushin' that diesel since early dawn
Ain't had no sleep, don't know how long
Whole lotta trouble takin' those curves
Gotta have a little somethin' to settle my nerves.
Well, hey, little waitress, make my coffee strong
A pack of king-sized filters and a country song
A little box of whities, help pick me up.
Caffein, nicotine, benzedrine,
And wish me luck.

Yeh, it's true that it's pretty rough on the independents these days. It's getting harder and harder to make it these days, and quitting is no easy matter. You hear stories all the time about someone leavin' trucking and buying a store. He'd work the place for a couple of years, seven days a week from 7 AM to 7 PM, until he started crawlin' up the walls. What's extra hard, though, is that in order to save their life, they're goin' to have to start complaining about it. You see, we're all kind of proud of the fact that we can push these rigs for hours, with not much sleep, too much coffee, pullin' eighty head of stinkin' cattle in a pouring rain, and still not complain about it. I mean we have this Paul Bunyan—or someone like that—image about ourselves. Most people think we are pretty low types anyway, and even though there are over a million truckers, most people don't even know one. They think of stories like, "You talk just like a truck driver," or something like that. Or else they see some guy on TV saying they make $37,000 a year. $37,000! Why some executives don't make that. The public thinks we're either bums or gettin' rich. Either way he thinks, "What do those guys want?" Even the best of us nets about $15,000 a year, and that doesn't take in account putting chains on in the middle of the night, blown-out tires, never seein' your families, and all that. It's a strange conflict. We want to save our reputation, but our reputation's not that good.

WBAP, DALLAS AND FORT WORTH

Before we play the next song from Conway Twitty, let me read a few more names. . . . I want to say hello to Linda Hanson from John Hanson calling from north-central Arkansas. . . . Hello to Bill from Dorothy in Dallas. . . . Dirty Dirty wanted a song played for Truman, one of the Hank Williams songs. . . . Folks, we've gotten 250 calls tonight, so I can't promise we'll get to them all. . . . and now, "I Can't See Me Without You."

WWVA, WHEELING, WEST VIRGINIA

For the past several years, the WWVA Wheeling Jamboree has put together a special truckers' show for its Labor Day Weekend Saturday night live radio broadcast, complete with trucker heavies, Dave Dudley, Dick Curles, and Red Sovine. Last year's two shows drew over 4,000 truckers, wives, girlfriends, and fans.

WWVA is talking about putting together a traveling truckers' show to work off the back of a semi or a flatbed and travel on the truck-stop circuit.

Wheeling Tunnel, Wheeling, West Virginia

That Old Highway Song

Well I pulled out of Pittsburgh rollin' down that
*   Eastern Seaboard,*
I got my diesel wound up and she's a-runnin' like
*   a-never before.*
There's a speed zone down ahead, well all right,
I don't see a cop in sight,
Six days on the road, and I'm gonna make it home tonight.

I got ten forward gears and a sweet Georgia overdrive,
I'm takin' little white pills and my eyes are open wide.
I just passed a Jimmy and a White,
I'm passing everything in sight,
Six days on the road, and I'm gonna make it home tonight.

My rig's a little old, but that don't mean she's slow,
There's a flame from her stack and that smoke's blowin'
*   black as coal,*
My hometown's comin' in sight,
And if you think I'm glad, you're right.
Six days on the road, and I'm gonna make it home tonight.

My banker told me to buy a bakery, buy a drugstore, buy anything but a truck because every hippie and teenager is easily gonna put me out of business. The return on the investment isn't high enough. Well, the pay isn't great. On an average trip with average pay and load, I make about $125. That's for two days' work. It comes to about 45–50 cents a mile. It all depends on what you're haulin', though. The big outfit drivers are somewhat different from the small ones. Besides having their high hats on, they make good money and have pretty easy rides. I made $500 a week working for them once. The highest I ever made in my life was $585 in one week, but that was for haulin' dynamite.

The main reason guys drive for freight lines is financial. There are less operational headaches, that's for sure. When you're finished with a run, you don't have to go home and wash the truck and do the bookkeeping. But there are also all sorts of restrictions. Some companies make you call in every night or they'll fine you ten dollars. It's the only way they can find their trucks.

Now, when you're drivin' somebody else's leased truck, you get 25 per cent of the load, and the owner gets 43 per cent. The carrier that owns the license gets the rest. If the carrier owns the trailer, then he gets 75 per cent, but he's got all the expenses.

It's really crazy drivin' for some company that's not a freight line. You usually have shorter runs, but you can begin to feel like a yo-yo—just like the load itself. There's a place in Pennsylvania. They ship sugar or something to Cincinnati. Me and a friend of mine used to work there for a while. On my way to Cincinnati, I'd pass him in another truck comin' from Cincinnati carrying the same stuff back to where I just came from. The only thing I could figure out was that they had to change the dates around a little bit.

I'm carrying newsprint these days. If I get down to New Orleans, I can get me a load of bananas. That pays a lot more than newsprint. Or grapefruit. You know, the freight on grapefruit is more than the cost of the grapefruit itself. I think, though, watermelon's about my favorite, even though it's expensive to load and unload them. If you give the guy five dollars, he'll throw thirty or forty extra watermelons on the truck. I get up around Chicago and sell 'em off for a dollar apiece.

It's a lot safer haulin' that stuff. Liquids slosh around and knock the rig back and forth every time you change gears. Jars you to shit. Cattle get caught, and they start moving so much they can tip a trailer. Steel and coils often crash right through the cab if you make a sudden stop. You have to go out and tighten the chains every fifty miles. Hardware, electronics, cigarettes, and whisky—they all get hijacked too often. A friend of mine was hijacked five or six years ago in Brooklyn. One or two blocks after he picked up his load, they cut him off and jumped him with guns on both sides. Joe's a big guy, but he was scared. These two guys had guns in his ribs. They threw him in the back of a Cadillac and put him on the floor while a big guy unloaded the truck. They didn't hurt him, though. Just took him to a warehouse and told him to keep his mouth shut. They were good Italian boys. They gave him a tuna sandwich, a pack of cigarettes, and a two-dollar tip, and didn't touch the $200 he had in his pocket.

On April 13, 1972, at 9 A.M. the northbound produce truck, traveling at an estimated speed of 55 mph, veered off the left side of the highway onto the 50-foot-wide grass median. It continued across the median, entered the opposing lanes, and collided with the left side of a southbound tank truck. The produce tractor caught fire and stopped in a jackknifed position against the right side of the trailer, blocking both southbound lanes. The tank truck, which had swerved left to avoid collision, ran off the left side of the highway onto the median. A southbound car that had been following the tank truck collided with the left side of the burning produce tractor. Both vehicles were engulfed in flames. The car driver, who was wearing a seat belt, escaped from the burning vehicle. However, the driver of the produce truck was trapped in the wreckage and suffered fatal burns. The driver of the tank truck and the car

The FBI sure bothered him though. They thought he was in on it, which happens every time any truck gets hijacked. They followed him and checked him out for years.

Of course all this doesn't include accidents. I've only been in two wrecks. Once my brakes failed going sixty miles per hour. I tried to glance off the trees on the side of the road but that didn't slow me down. Finally I saw a cemetery up ahead, and I plowed right into it. . . . I went over half the tombstones before the truck stopped.

Over on 71 last year, they had a big flood. The road goes under an underpass and got flooded out. The road crews built up some sort of dams under the road to buckle it up a bit. I was haulin' a double and I got to the bridge. I was supposed to have two or three inches of clearance, but the dams raised the pavement up about six inches. I came in there about fifty miles per hour and ripped the top off both trailers like I was opening a sardine can. The state paid for the two trailers and repaired that bridge pretty quick.

Back in 1970, Tri-state was trying to break the union. They got this old boy who was down and out to haul this load of black powder. Some asshole put a 30/06 into the side of the trailer and the son of a bitch blew up. It left a hole thirty feet deep and fifty feet across in the middle of Interstate 44 outside of Springfield. I hear it broke windows fifteen miles away. They say that all they ever found of the ole boy was part of his right foot.

driver suffered relatively minor injuries. The accident resulted in one fatality, two injuries, and $15,000 property damage.

Laboratory tests taken two hours after the accident disclosed a high percentage of amphetamines in the driver's system. According to the physician who performed the tests, the driver may have "hallucinated" and tried to avoid a nonexistent oncoming vehicle.

—from *Overdrive* magazine

I'm drivin' a truck on a mountain road,
Got a hot-rod rig and I'm flyin' low,
My eyes are filled with diesel smoke,
And them hairpin curves, they ain't no joke.
Diesel smoke and dangerous curves.

Out last night, drinkin' beer with the guys,
Got an achin' head and bloodshot eyes,
Ended with a pretty little dame,
I can't even remember her name.
Diesel smoke and dangerous curves.

I guess I closed my eyes awhile,
Here I am, I'm runnin' wild,
I burned my brakes, I stripped my gears,
I gotta ride her down I fear.
Diesel smoke and dangerous curves.

I should'a left them women alone.
It's too late now, I think I'm gone.
Gotta get myself outta this fix,
'Cause I know now you just can't mix
Diesel smoke and dangerous curves.

Texas-Oklahoma line, I-35

Evanston, Wyoming

Loveland Pass, Colorado

Elko, Nevada

I usually drive at night. That's less traffic and the truck runs better. Even though in some states the speed limits are lower, they usually don't bother you if the traffic ain't heavy. That is, except for Ohio. They bother you in Ohio any time. But even though the drivin' is better, nighttime is when you begin to feel strange, away from your family. It's not loneliness so much as you just want to feel something, have somebody reach over and touch you. Your eyes start to play tricks on you. I've seen flying saucers in the desert in Nevada. Going into San Jose—I think it's 17 up there—I thought I saw army maneuvers up and down the road when all it was were trees.

I was in Louisiana or Alabama—somewhere down there—going from one town to another that's real close to each other. I saw a bunch of elephants walking down the highway with blinker lights on their tails. I stopped this guy in the next town and told him what I saw. I asked him if he saw them too. He looked at me funny and said, "No, you just take too many pills." I found out later that there was a circus in one town and the elephants were walking to the next town because the circus was moving. They wore blinker lights down the highway so that nobody would run into them. If I hadn't of found that out I would've packed it in.

One young trucker told me, "I tried some dexies once, but I started having hallucinations and nightmares. It wasn't worth it, so I quit." I knew one guy who would take pills and he kept on seeing trains crossing the highway, so he'd pull up and stop. Then one time he decided he wouldn't stop. He should have.

Well, I haul my rig out of San Jose.
I better be in Cincinnati Monday morning for to draw my pay.
I can't waste no time in this all-night grill,
So I jumped in my Jimmy,
And popped a few little white pills.

Well, here I sit
All alone with a broken heart.
About two or three bennies,
And my semi truck won't start.

Winnemucca, Nevada

Father, mother, son, and fiancée

The guys that miss their families and go home for a week or so start to go crazy. They just have to get back on the road. Even though they begin to wonder if their wife's cheating on 'em, and the wife begins to worry about why he starts bringing two pairs of clothes with him, it's the way that kind of life is. I read a survey of truckers' wives called "Horny or Holy." It said 25 per cent of them cheat on their husbands. The best way to do this thing is do it alone, 'cause it takes a special kinda marriage.

There was this guy named Bill Strongberg. He was a good old boy. Got killed in Nevada a couple of years ago near Silver Springs. He fell asleep at the wheel and his truck rolled over. He was a good man. . . . I used to ride with him. I used to pick him up at his house and he and his wife would always have the same conversation.

He'd say, "Honey, if I don't make it home, we've had a good life together."

She'd look him right in the eye and tell him, "Bill, you son of a bitch, you've got that fire in that truck and you're gonna take it to Las Vegas."

They both would laugh. They really loved each other. But that's special. I think the problem is why a lot of wives are drivin' with their husbands these days. They can't give up either life.

Ain't got time to play the pinball
or get the radar blues
Gotta keep these big wheels rollin'
I'm a-comin' home to you.
I know my baby's waiting
the sweetest I ever seen
With big blue eyes that sparkle
she's a truck driver's queen.

I was ridin' my thumb out across the state
A truck pulled up and hit them big air brakes
Got outside Abilene, met Big Bertha
The truck driver's queen.
She shook my hand and put her glove back on
Jumped on the gears like a dog on a bone
Wad of chaw tobacco bulgin' in her mouth
Grabbed a handful of wheel and whipped that big truck south
At eighty miles an hour I was really gettin' scared
It's hard to believe that she was still grabbin' gears
Read a meter at a hundred and three,
She missed the stick and grabbed my knee
Oh Big Bertha, Bertha the truck drivin' queen.

TRUCK DRIVER'S WIFE

Before I started drivin' with my husband, I was told it was no place for a woman . . . that I wouldn't be able to handle the cab, change tires, load and unload. Well that's true, but I don't have to do that when I drive with him. There are other considerations. The busiest month we had, he did 70,000 miles without getting out of the truck. He did it by himself. No help. That's a long time away from your home, and hard on your family. So I drive with him, mainly because it's the only way for us to be together.

Our kids are three, four, and five, and he takes them sometimes. Our five-year-old has been in Montana, Arizona, Colorado—just about all the Western states. It gives them a chance to be alone with their dad. They don't have kindergarten in Idaho, so the five-year-old missed school last year by two weeks and spends lots of time with his dad. It's good for them to see lots of country. The kids do real well and never fuss in the truck. They enjoy it and sleep well. Travelin' a different road every day keeps the monotony out. It's a good life, and we make a good livin' at it.

I do it more to see my husband—sort of out of self-defense —but we have friends that really drive as a team, coast to coast. She only takes enough time off to take care of the bookwork that's necessary. The rest of the time she's on the truck.

The truck stops are becomin' more aware of the woman trucker as far as havin' her own store, showers, and whatnot. Before you had to stand outside the men's shower and take a chance. They're payin' more attention to the food now, instead of the usual garbage.

The kids always talk of being truckers when they grow up. The oldest is going to drive a big rig, and the three-year-old will drive a potato-chip truck 'cause he's smaller.

SATIN AND STEEL BY MONTI TAK, WOMAN TRUCKER

Few of my fellow truckers realize the obstacles a woman trucker must overcome to perform the same duties they do. How would you feel if you weren't admitted to a plant for hours on end, while the guards and a few petty officials hemmed and hawed and passed the buck? When you *are* admitted, you are accompanied by an armed guard, not to protect your person from harm, but to protect their precious steel plant, ostensibly from *you!* You are treated like a foreign spy whose every move is highly suspect, and subjected to judgment and criticism from a bunch of ignorant dockhands.

You are a qualified driver, trained for your job by an exacting owner-operator who let you cut your teeth on his Mack Triplex. You have had a five-year-old obsession with being the best trucker possible. You think no more of driving from New York to Chicago than most women think of running down to the shopping center, and yet, and yet. . . . How would you feel if you applied for an over-the-road job and the interviewer said, "Well, you passed all your written and road tests exceptionally well, but we've never hired a man with brown eyes before." Just substitute the word "woman" for "man with brown eyes" and maybe you can comprehend the frustration and bitterness of discrimination.

Discrimination is displayed by many more people than just potential employers. Truck stops and waitresses sometimes also discriminate. All too often I have sat in the "Truckers Only" section of a restaurant in order to get fast service, only to have the waitresses ignore my presence, or to ask me to sit in the open section "with the other tourists."

Other truckers discriminate when they fail to judge women truckers as individuals and make sweeping generalizations about their ability, mentality, and knowledge. I am very thankful for the courteous truckers who are kind enough to reserve judgment. I don't mind those who resent me as long as they leave me alone and let us go our separate ways. I do mind those who think I can't even read the dipstick or check my own tires and load without their almighty help and advice. When I need help, I'll ask for it.

Many people want to know why I chose to drive a truck. If you know what trucking is, I don't have to explain it to you, because it's in your blood. This is what makes it difficult to convey my feelings to people who have little or no knowledge about the trucking industry.

Certainly it isn't for the money. I'd love to know why the public thinks truckers are a blue-collar version of the Vanderbilts (perhaps because we can pay off a $25,000 rig in three or four years when it takes twenty to pay off a house of the same cost).

Yeah, there's getting to be a lot more women truckers. If they handle the job, I say more power to 'em. I know this one freight company in Texas has a woman driver and they painted her rig purple.

—male truckdriver

I enjoy traveling and seeing new sights and faces. Like most truckers, I feel closed in if I work indoors, and the politics of the office has never appealed to me.

Today's world is dominated by the Group Man; individualism is rare and often regarded as abnormal. A sense of self-worth, pride in one's chosen profession, and the ability to earn one's own way are certainly characteristic of many other creative professions. The owner-operator typifies the individual who best exists in a freely competitive society, where monetary reward is gained on the basis of achievement and not on the judgment of the Welfare Board. Like most drivers, I like being independent and my own boss.

Now, years after I first sat behind the wheel, I have made into reality things that were once only aspirations and pipe dreams. I have seen things and done more real living than many people over twice my age. I have friends all over the country, a job I love, and a rig I'm proud to own.

I like being able to feel the wind in my face and to see the sun come up. When I hear the scream of a diesel on the night wind, I know I wouldn't be happy anywhere else. Despite all the odds against the trucker, when there's a good load on the trailer, and that 318 is putting out the most beautiful music in the world, I wouldn't trade places with anyone.

She was a truck drivin' woman
How she moved, oh yah.
She pulled a rig out of Richmond
Just ridin' a big old Diamond-T truck
But I never think of puttin' her down
'Cause you just don't mess with women
Who drive trucks around.

A Little Place Called Hamburger Inn

I stopped at a roadhouse in Texas
A little place called Hamburger Inn.
I heard that old jukebox a-moanin'
A tune called The Truck Drivin' Man.

The waitress then brought me some coffee.
I thanked her, then called her again.
I said this here tune sure does fit me,
'Cause I'm a truck drivin' man.

Pour me another cup of coffee,
For it is the best in the land.
I'll put a nickel in the jukebox
And play The Truck Drivin' Man.

I climbed back aboard my old semi,
And then like a flash I was gone.
I got them old truck wheels a-rollin'
I'm on my way to San Antone.

When I get my call up in glory
They'll take me away from this land.
I'll herd my old truck up to heaven
'Cause I'm a truck drivin' man.

A HOME AWAY FROM HOME
FLAGSTAFF, Ariz. (AP)—The truck driver calls her over. His three buddies in the booth are laughing. He has a dirty story to tell. Jean, somewhere over 40, her trim waitress figure hiding in the white pants suit, her grey hair frozen with spray, squeezes into the booth. "Hey, girls," she calls. "He's got a story." The other two waitresses hover, smiling, expectant.

The truck driver begins a tale about a salesman with a lisp. Jean's head falls lightly. "Ah, you've heard it before," the truck driver says. "Go ahead. *They* haven't," she says. The story tumbles to its unfortunate conclusion, not very funny, not very dirty, but everyone laughs anyway.

The laughter gives brief life to the nearly empty diner.

Jean has been a waitress so long, few stories are new any more. The drivers and their small talk float in from the highway and out again. Jean remains, purveyor of coffee and smiles, beneficiary of the larger tip, recorder of their passing this way. She is one of the family at this truck stop, a very temporary family in a very temporary home.

The road sign says Beaton Truck Plaza, about halfway between New Mexico and the California desert. Open 24 hours. The light-towers over the gas pumps break the burden of the night. The windows of the diner frame a stereoscopic scene. Empty booths, waitresses waiting, clock standing still, a driver staring at his orange juice, the cook immobile against the stainless steel backdrop. From a distance, toys in a lighted box. Seven miles west of town.

The American truck stop. It conjures up romantic fictions. Marilyn Monroe beguiling a lonesome cowhand at a bus stop in a small town. Humphrey Bogart as killer Duke Mantee terrorizing the Black Mesa Filling Station and Bar B-Q on an Arizona highway, from Robert Sherwood's *The Petrified Forest*.

Sherwood set the stage with stark reality: "a lunch counter, with cash register, ketchup bottles, toothpicks, chewing gum and Life-Saver rack, cigars, cigarettes." Truck stops share a kind of mystery, a kind of excitement, a place for something to happen where nothing happens. Haven for strangers, a way station. Something of the Pony Express, the stage-coach.

Through these doors walk the best gearjammers in the world.

> *—sign on a truck stop door*

Q: Do you have a *Time* magazine?

A: No, we just carry those girlie magazines to keep the dirty old truck drivers happy.

> *—at a truck stop newsstand*

Ravishing Ruby, she's been around for a while
Ravishing Ruby, she was a truck-stop child
Born in the back of a rig somewhere near L. A.
Ravishing Ruby, you've poured a lot of hot coffee in your day.

Ravishing Ruby believes anything you say
Just like her daddy said, said he'd be back someday
She was just fourteen, she grew up wild and free
And all the time she's been waitin' on him
She's been waitin' on you and me.

Ravishing Ruby, she sleeps in a bunk out back
Her days and nights are filled with a man named Smilin' Jack
That was her daddy's name, and that's all she ever knew
Ravishing Ruby ain't got time for guys like me and you.

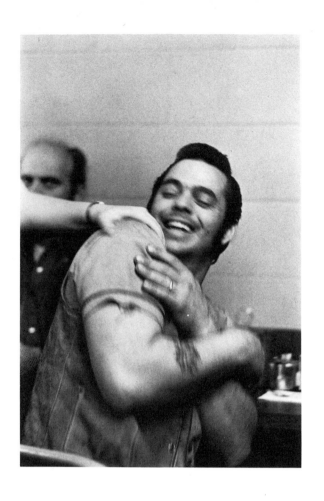

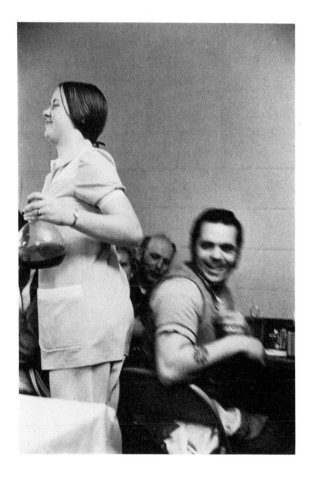

Only the vehicles have changed, to quicken the pace, haul the oil and explosives, hurry the strawberries and tomatoes from California's San Joaquin Valley to Cleveland, Ohio. The unchanging roadside tribute: "See all the trucks parked there, Mary? That means the food is good. They know where to stop."

But the romance aside, the truck stop is more often a mecca on a map, 400 miles ahead, measured by the appetite of the truck for fuel, the gullet for food, the eyes for sleep, and the stiffness in the back and legs. It is also a convenience, quick service, and a chance for a few hours with people you know after a day with only yourself.

So it is this night, at this small oasis perched on the concrete edge of an American artery.

The sun forces the daylight temperatures to 110 degrees on the Arizona desert, so some drivers prefer to roll at night. Two of them have taken a dinner break. It is after 11. The head driver twists toward his plate and grumbles, "Let's get goin' while its cool."

Southern accent, a voice strangely small and quiet for the big frame from which it comes, large forearms and fading tattoos. He and his partner have been pushing the double trailer rig from Kansas westward. He finishes and goes out to sign the credit card receipt for 125 gallons of diesel oil. The truck jerks to a start and the high torque of the engine grinds toward the white staccato of the centerline US 66, and a noisy race with the Atchison, Topeka, and Santa Fe, running parallel 300 feet south.

I guess it's the idea of a home away from home. You have Western Union, and showers and phones, a place to wash up and shave, to do some laundry. And it's very clean.

Upstairs, beyond a sign that says "Truckers Only," there are a sofa, a television set, two easy chairs, pool table, and small rooms that rent for $4 a night, just a bed, but a place to stretch out without doubling the knees, away from the groaning engine. Still a trucker on his own pocket prefers to nap in the tractor, parked in the lot, the engine going to keep up the air conditioning.

The trucks are there in force in the early morning, again in the evening. The large rigs line up in the lot in military order, wearing their license plates on the grills like campaign ribbons: Arizona, Nevada, Utah, California, Kansas, Illinois, Ohio. Pennsylvania.

The crew of 45 that works this truck stop pumps an average of 10,000 gallons of diesel fuel a day. Two diesel mechanics are ready to hit the road at a moment's notice, equipped to do a complete overhaul at roadside. At morning and dusk it looks and sounds like a World War II airfield

with the heavy bombers landing one by one, the ground crews swarming over the hot engines, the scarred windshields.

On a window facing the truck side of the lot is a poster proclaiming, "$5,000 Reward. Gurney Oil Co., Memphis, Tenn . . . for information leading to the recovery of . . ." Following is a detailed description and pictures of a truck-trailer combination with close-ups of its special equipment. Stolen: "Jan. 17, 1971 . . . Call Collect."

Of course, companionship is one of the major reasons for truck stops. Certainly, the food isn't any big attraction. You can get all your needs serviced there. They'll bail you out if you get a ticket. Most of the big ones have hot lines to the shipping brokers. Some of them are like mini-shopping centers, and some are Ma and Pa all the way. They're really the only stopping place most truckers get to go to, so they better be able to fill every desire, 'cause the word gets around. Truckers can make or break those places.

The Pavement Princess

Well, woman, don't you put no bets on me
That I might settle down,
'Cause I'm just not the settlin' kind,
I've gotta chase around.
Well I'm a truck drivin' daddy,
And I keep on goin',
And it's just about time that I'm gone.
Black smoke blowin' over 18 wheels,
Well, honey, that's my home.
Black smoke blowin' over 18 wheels
Is the only home I've ever known.

You know, Vicki was like a little kid the first time I hooked up with her.

She said, "Hell, I've been fuckin' truckers for the past three years and I never been in a truck. Now I'm goin' to."

She went with me on Sunday and we came back Monday night. We had some rough road and before too long her tits would flop up and down. She got sore as hell. I guess that's why there aren't more women drivers.

Vicki has two places. Never did have much trouble with the one downtown. She's got doors, a buzzer, two-way mirrors, and a guy who knows all the plainclothes cops and detectives. He knows who to let in and who not to let in. But the cops usually let you know beforehand when they're gonna have a raid. The state police can't bust you inside the city limits without a warrant. But not at a truck stop. That's a business place. . . . Anyone can walk in there. That's how they get the truck stops. The last time they raided Vicki's it was an $11,000 bond. Tried to make a believer out of her that they wanted that truck stop closed. I think it was mainly because a lot of young kids and businessmen started coming to the stop. But they never bother the guys. They just take in the girls, book 'em, and put 'em back to work in a half hour.

You know, a lot of them have good protection. One night I was at this truck stop that was a whorehouse and the sheriff comes in. I seen when he pulled up front and went back and told the girls. They went upstairs, went out the bathroom window and out on the roof just as he was coming in. The woman who took care of the girls left too, so he came over to me and wanted to know who ran the place. I just played dumb and said, "Hell, I don't know. I stopped in here to get a cup of coffee."

He said, "Well, I'll tell you what. Things better slow down around here or I'll be back."

I said, "If anyone comes in I'll tell 'em before I leave."

He left and I went and got the girls back. It just happens that a guy from Cleveland comes down that night with a couple of girls. I told him the story and he said that he would fix that. I don't know who he called, but he asked me to describe what this guy looked like while he was on the phone. He must have been talkin' to the sheriff's department, 'cause he told everybody that the officer was just a rookie and just got out of school two weeks ago, but that everyone should go back to work and not worry 'cause that guy had just lost his job.

I'll tell you, they're not kidding when they say they're open twenty-four hours with round-the-clock service.

I can't see where prostitution hurts a thing. I'd rather see it in a place like that where it's clean and they go to the doctor. I won't mess with 'em when they're down hustling outside a truckstop. Hell, you don't know what you're gonna run into knockin' on the doors of your truck. . . .

I was in a rest area with no facilities over in Frederick, Maryland. I'd been to Philadelphia and had Vicki with me. She never did work on Sunday nights. I stopped to take a leak outside the truck when a queer come up. I guess he wasn't figurin' on anyone being in the truck with me.

He said, "Can I help you?"

I said, "No, don't think I need any help."

He said, "Well, I'd sure be obliged to help you."

Vicki rolled down the window. "By God," she said, "you heard him. If he needs any help, then I'll do it."

He cut a trail.

Up Route 23 through Ohio, this queer passed me blinkin' his lights. I thought it was a woman. He had long blonde hair and it was at night. He blinked his lights and I blinked mine. Still thought it was a woman. I turned at a stop and he got out and came over to the truck. I rolled down the windows. He asked if he could help me and I told him, no, I don't think so. Hell, some will follow you twelve to fifteen miles, dressed in earrings, blinkin' their lights.

Hitchhikers can get you in trouble too. I wasn't fifteen miles from home one evening, so I called the old lady and told her to have supper for me at 9 o'clock. I picked up this girl who was hitchhiking. She got in and I thought she was goin' downtown where I was going, but I asked her where she was going.

"Any place you're going," she said.

I told her to crawl back in the sleeper and drop the curtain, and not to stick her head out if I stopped to talk to anybody. I figured it could possibly cause a run-in with my old lady. I drove on through town and I got to a little town on the other side where I could stop and call my wife. I told her they just changed my schedule and I had to go down to Mississippi to get a load.

This little gal had been drinking and I figured that next morning, when she sobered off, she'd be ready to get out. We went to a motel and stayed 'till the next morning. When we got up I said,

"Say, where'd you say you're goin' to?"

She said, "Any place you're goin'. I'm with you."

I took her to a truck stop, and when she went to the restroom, I went out and jumped in the truck and took off. Funny thing was that in the lot there was a one of those religious groups that holds services from a tractor-trailer at truck stops.

I picked up this broad hitchhiking one night. I hadn't gone fifty miles and she started pullin' her clothes off. It was about a hundred degrees in the sleeper so I grabbed the blanket and pillow—just gettin' ready to do it right there on the Interstate. But she didn't go for that. I had just dropped a load of swingin' beef and was runnin' empty, so I told her about the readymade air conditioner in the trailer, so we jumped back there and did it.

Give me those girls in the houses. They go to the doctor once a week. They check everybody. Wash 'em down. Very seldom do you ever hear of somebody catchin' anything from 'em. Always pay cash though. I made the mistake once of cashing a personal check. They got my name and called my old lady. That's how she found out I was messing around.

VICE COST ME MY FAMILY

My name is Jerry Brewer and I'm like many truckers who get the air of independence by being their own boss behind the wheel and having deep convictions that following the white strip down the highway is the only way of life. I found myself being contrary to the upbringing of my family and doing like many of my fellow truckers. I began to chase the women, use language that is unbecoming to a gentleman and, in short, the longer I ran the roads, the deeper I found myself in the vices that deprived me of true happiness.

Such was the case when I fell in love and married the girl of my choice and had two lovely children. The open road and the ever present corruption that was found alongside of it caused me to lose both my children and my home. This drove me almost to the breaking point and in desperation I called out to God. I promised Him if He would let me have my children back, I would raise them to know Him and would also live for Him.

Praise God, He gave me the children and I too have kept my promise to Him. The Lord saved me and filled me with His Spirit.

They told Vicki about it. Me and her were gonna have to cool things. She said not to worry about it and just laughed.

One night I pulled into Calumet Pier in Chicago. I don't know how that guy knew me. I walked in and sat down to drink some coffee. This guy sat down behind me and said he had a message for me. He even called me by name.

"You and Vicki better cool it. You either leave your old lady and move in with her or you stay the hell out of Wheeling."

I snuck right out of there. Everything was fine when I finally left my old lady.

I don't get back to Wheeling much. I would if they gave me a load. Vicki's Mom and Dad are out there. They've got an $80,000 home. Last time I was there, I got in about midnight. Her folks were really glad to see me. They asked me if I was here to stay. I said, no, I was just passing through.

Vicki's Mom turned to her and said, "Didn't I tell you? That's just like a goddamn truck driver. All he wants is what he can get out of you."

Yes, my trucking buddy, I do know what it is to almost lose my family and to attempt suicide, for I had nothing to live for. But today as I travel over the highways, I do so with joy in my heart because Christ has forgiven me of my sins and has filled me with His power to overcome all temptations. Why not try God's way today?
　　—from
　　Highway Evangelist

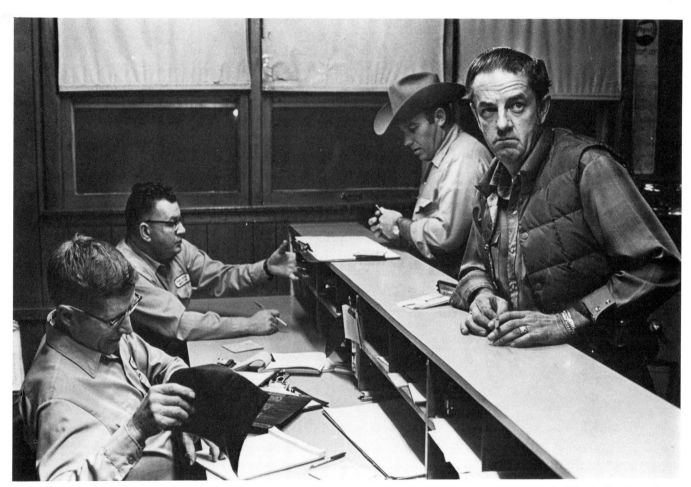

Port of entry, New Haven, Kansas

The ICC's a-Checkin' on Down the Line

The ICC is a-checkin' on down the line
I'm a little overweight and my logbook's way behind,
But nothing bothers me tonight,
I can dodge all the scales all right.
Six days on the road, and I'm gonna make it home tonight.

We're all crazy when we drive a truck to begin with, but if we know we're crazy, we're not too crazy to drive one. And next to the various state regulations, commissions, and rules, we seem like the sanest men that ever lived. Each state has its own particular way of dealing with truckers, each different enough to keep you guessing. And each state has developed its own special ways to harass the drivers.

Ohio has got to be the worst. It is known as "the Gestapo state." If I go through Ohio, I just plan on getting a ticket. Any little light broken, any little minor infraction, they'll get you and fine you heavy. You can be fined $500 for not wearing a seat belt. The highway patrol has mirrors on a long pole which they stick up to the cab windows. They say, "Keep your hands on the steering wheel until I see if you've got your seat belt on." They've got a radar that's like a gun. They just point it at you and it will pick up your speed. Any bit over the speed limit and you won't get very far. Sixty-one or sixty-two miles per hour and they'll nab you. The state makes a lot of money on that, and, hell, the roads ain't that good.

God, I hate that state. The last time I got a ticket there I called the cop everything in the book. I was anxious to get to this one truck stop, get me a cup of coffee, and wash my face. I saw the stop up ahead so I picked it up to seventy. This cop pulled me over and accused me of being drunk. I did look like I was in bad shape. He said, "That'll be twenty-five dollars." I cussed him and the State of Ohio. I've gotten five tickets there, and that's the only place I ever get tickets. Last April a cop stopped me and asks me if I've got twenty-five dollars. I said no. He said that if I didn't have it, I was goin' to jail. I said, "Let me dig into my billfold. I think I can come up with something pretty fast."

New Mexico still does that sort of thing if they want to. New Mexico is like runnin' in a foreign country. They have things hidden away that guys don't even know exist until they drop 'em on you. They have these cute hidden laws and rules and regulations they can spring on you at the least bit of provocation. It doesn't take much to provoke them either. I know a guy that was fined a hundred and twenty-five dollars for not having a first-aid kit in his truck. Okay, so he goes and buys a first-aid kit, and the next trip coming back they nailed him again because it wasn't up to New Mexico standards, which meant it wasn't an official New Mexico first-aid kit.

Won't you shake hands, buddy, with a truck drivin' man
A-runnin' from the coast to the southern land
Hit the Smoky Mountains, but I have no fear
Air brakes a-screamin' and I'm fightin' with the gears.

Got a load of freight out of New Orleans
Tryin' to miss the scales into Tennessee.
A fifty-dollar fine would nearly kill my soul
A-eatin' up the profit on my doggone load.

The goin' gets hard, ah, nobody knows
The road patrol's hungry so he flagged me off the road
He said I was speedin' by his radar scan
Speedin' up a hill with an overloaded van.

#392.65 Sleeper berth. Transfer to or from. No person shall transfer to or from a sleeper berth while a motor vehicle is in motion.

#393.95 Reflecting elements. Each reflecting element or surface shall meet the requirement for a red Class A reflector contained in the SAE Recommended Practice "Reflex Reflectors." The aggregate candlepower output of all the reflecting elements or surface in one direction shall not be less than 12 when tested in a perpendicular position with observation at one-third degree as specified in the Photometric Test contained in the above-mentioned Recommended Practice.

#395.8 Driver's daily log. The total hours in each duty status must be entered and submitted daily: Off duty other than in a sleeper berth; off duty in a sleeper berth; driving; and on duty not driving shall be entered, the total of which entries shall equal 24 hours.

—from *The Red Book: The Motor Carrier Safety Regulations Handbook*

The average weight of a loaded truck is 73,280 pounds, and when I say 73,280 pounds, that's what I mean, 'cause 73,281 pounds and you're fined. You drive through Iowa in a snowstorm and pick up another five or six hundred pounds of snow. You have to pay for the snow. You pull up on the scale and they say you're overloaded. You can explain that it's because of the snow and they'll say, "Take it up with God." Poor God gets blamed for lots of things.

In Arizona, they've got the ACC, yet another commerce commission. They come around and check you all the time. They'll stop you and check your logbooks, even pull you out of the sleeper, even though it's illegal to check you when you're off duty. There was a guy who was stopped by an ACC man. He started checkin' his log and then asked to see the co-driver's log also. The driver told him he couldn't do that because that was his wife in the sleeper and there wasn't any way he was gonna let him look back there. The ACC guy started to get into the cab anyway, and the driver reached up and whacked him between the eyes with a tire iron and killed him on the spot. The sheriff let him go because it was a justifiable homicide.

In Mississippi, you have to buy thirty-one gallons of fuel whether you need it or not. And you don't get out of the state until you show this ignorant redneck slob—and I'm being kind callin' him that—sitting in his booth with his little window, your receipt for buying that fuel.

You know, you can cross out to Canada easier and cheaper than goin' into California just by buying a twenty-five-dollar permit. Mexico is the same way. You can't even buy a permit for Missouri.

And then there's the various fees and licenses and permits that you have to pay. That's the original Pandora's box. Even if you pay for your own rig, you have to cough up permit fees for each state you drive in, which can run you about $5,700 a year. A base plate is going to cost you $1,000 right there. That's just for one state. On top of that you've got your prorate. The one particular state you're based in has a prorate agreement with other states. It keeps you from having to buy more than one base plate, but it enables the other states you travel in to collect from you even when you're just driving in your home state.

Some states charge you a ton-mile tax and others charge you a wheel tax based on your total mileage through that state. If you bought a trip permit for Wyoming, it would cost you $22.85 to go from Laramie to Evanston.

THE INDEPENDENT CONTRACTOR:
—selects, hires, directs, and fires drivers and helpers.
—pays workmen's compensation, deducts social security, and pays fringe benefits (if any) for drivers and helpers.
—sets working conditions and hours for drivers or helpers.
—pays liability and cargo insurance.
—is responsible for cargo damage.
—purchases license plates, permits, fuel-tax permits.
—pays for all operating and maintenance costs.
—is allowed to have his own name, as well as the carrier, on the equipment.
—controls the loading and unloading of the cargo.
—determines when he will operate (within the limits required by the customer).
—determines the speed to be traveled as well as the routes.
—is responsible for damage to the equipment.
—does not have to give progress reports or duty call-ins beyond what the ICC or state laws require.
—does not have to pay any fines imposed by carriers for failure to call in.
—can refuse loads and otherwise haul when and where he wants to.
  —from *Overdrive* magazine

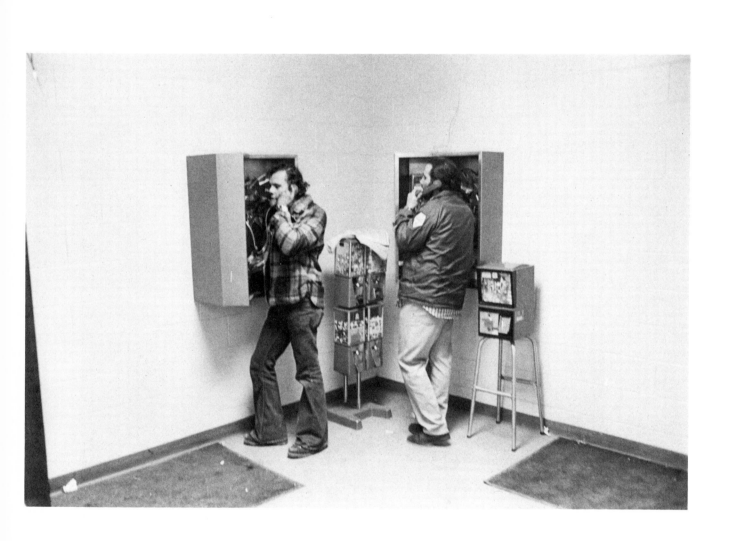

Port of entry, New Haven, Kansas

I know they just sit up nights dreaming of ways to get us, but truckers sit up nights dreaming of how not to get caught. That's where the citizen-band radios come in handy.

You have to pick up a lot of little tricks to survive. It used to be that you could get a big part of your tolls cut down on the Pennsylvania Turnpike by finding someone coming the other way and switch with him. They'd never check anything but the time, but now they put your wheel number on the toll sheet. Most scales weigh one axle at a time. Drivers have this way of jerking their load over the other axle, and back and forth, so they can be overloaded without showing it on the scale meter. Most of the operators don't even notice unless it goes way over anyway. But if they do, I always try to carry a case or two of whatever I'm carrying for the port of entry guys. That trick doesn't do you much good if you're haulin' limestone. Then you have to shell out a few dollars.

Usually I weigh myself before I get on. If I'm legal, I tell them to kiss my ass. If they want to argue, I'll just let them take me to see the judge, 'cause he'll come out and look at the scale. If I'm running close, I'll make sure I'm almost out of fuel. That's 800 pounds right there. There's this guy known as "Ole Red." He'd pull into entry points when he was carrying nothing just to drive those guys crazy. He'd pull up to the scales, get out of his truck, and start pounding all over his trailer with a little hammer. The operator would come out and ask him what the hell he was doing. Red would start at him real good and tell him that he thought he was overloaded, but was carrying a load of canaries and he wanted to get them all into the air before he got weighed.

CITIZEN-BAND RADIO

Blazer, Blazer, you got Smokey Bear sittin' in the plaza. That's his stand. He lives there.

Boy, let me know when that Smokey gets past the back door.

Smokey the Bear sittin' in the median. Go ahead, Jelly Bean. Watch it to the bridge, watch it, there's gonna be another comin' up behind you.

I'm goin' down that road feelin' bad
'cause my trailer come unhitched from my cab.

I'm lookin' for a job at honest pay,
no 18 hours and little white pills all day.

Sing me a truck-drivin' song
to drive away my blues when I'm gone.

Nebraska sunset

You've got to use your brains and be dishonest sometimes to stay ahead in this game. I've known guys to burn heating oil and kerosene in GMC diesel engines. They've got to forge receipts for fuel for the state compliance reports. They'll go into a truck stop and buy some fuses or maybe even a belt buckle and add some numbers on to the receipt. Why else would they spend $4.98 on a belt buckle to hold up a pair of $3.00 pants? Or else they just steal a blank receipt pad and fill them in themselves. Some guys will even fill in their own truck registrations and licensing tags. They'll use their car plates on their trailers, switch loads with other drivers, even intentionally break scales—anything to beat out the regulatory agencies and keep them from driving them into bankruptcy.

These agencies, they're regulatory nationally, but only for truck safety. The ICC checks your truck from head to toe—lights, air pressure, leak-warning systems, air hoses, seat belts, tires, even under the trailer. They literally check you all over, which is good. Trucks are a lot safer now than they used to be. But why is that the only thing done efficiently? I've been tryin' to figure out where the ICC fits into all this for years. It's the great mystery of trucking. It's a railroad agency that controls freight rates, but there's another regulator called the Department of Transportation. And then there's the Federal Highway Administration, then the Bureau of Motor Carrier Safety, and the Public Utility Commission. And still nothing is uniform. It's not all that pleasant. A truck legal in one state is not legal in another. And in the end, what it means to me is money, time, effort, and livelihood. Those are big things, you know.

There Ain't No Easy Run

White line fever
A sickness born down deep within my soul
White line fever
The years keep flying by like the highline poles.

The wrinkles on my forehead show the miles I've
        put behind me
They continue to remind me how fast I'm growing old
Guess I'll die with this fever in my soul.

I wonder just what makes a man keep pushin' on
Why must I keep on singing this old highway song
I've been from coast to coast a hundred times or more
And I ain't seen one single place where I ain't been before.

I usually don't get upset. We've always been hassled one way or another and we learn to live with it. It's just that I'm afraid for the independents—the little man who's been in the industry all his life and doesn't know anything else. How are they gonna rehabilitate all those people? They'll take 'em out of the trucks and tell 'em to go into farmin'. You're talkin' about probably 400,000 people whose life-style would be destroyed.

It's not like the old days when, even though you were independent, you could count on the union to help your basic situation. The Teamsters seem to work against us these days. Fitzsimmons is always coming out of meetings with Nixon saying there's nothing to worry about, everything is fine. There's a lot of people represented by Teamsters who don't like their representation. He certainly doesn't represent me. Lots of guys liked Hoffa better. Maybe he was a grafter and all that, but when he went to prison, there wasn't a union or nonunion person who didn't remember the three-and-a-half-cent-a-mile days, that the fact that they were getting sixteen cents now is due directly to Hoffa.

But the Teamsters don't give a damn about the rank and file now. I can get my roof caved in for saying that to certain elements of the Teamsters, but it's nonetheless true. They couldn't care less. This guy John Ford is fifty-seven years old and has been drivin' for thirty-five years. He would have retired a few years ago, but when his kids grew up he and his wife moved to a smaller place. He had to change locals and lost all his seniority and pension credits. He couldn't get another company job 'cause the big outfits retire you at fifty-five, so he bought his own rig and leased it out to a mobile-home-moving outfit. He had to start all over again.

A lot of guys carry a union card that are owner-operators just because they are leased to a company that also has general freight commodities like ICX, Navajo, PIE, Consolidated Freightways. These companies have their special commodity divisions where the guys haul meat, produce, beer, and other non-general-freight stuff. The union has really put the blocks on the independent here, forcing him to join the union and pay union dues in order to work. How can you not be suspicious of a trucking union that's in so many places they don't belong, from the ski slopes in Colorado to hotels in Miami Beach?

Independents just have to do their own fighting. The problem is that a truck is a politician's dream. It is something that can be taxed, but it can't vote. Two-thirds of every road paved in this country was bought and paid for with truck revenue, and still there's not a state government, not a federal agency that isn't sitting around figurin' some way to get more money out of the American trucker.

The truck driver as American culture hero—hah! He's Don Quixote all right, but instead of chargin' windmills, he charges bureaucracies. He could be so free, like I always dreamed. Workin' hard but havin' fun. And all he has to show for it is a thick book of government regulations that tells him he can't blow his nose unless he does it in the right direction.

We the people of the United States of America do hereby petition the government of the United States of America to correct the inequities of our present laws. We are hereby presenting a list of the 10 most pressing issues. They are as follows:

1. Speed limit to 60 or 65 mph.
2. Price rollback of gasoline prices to May 1973.
3. Complete public audit of oil industry reserves both at home and abroad.
4. Removal of allocation quotas from all truck stops.
5. Uniform regulations on the interstates.
6. Uniform regulations in all the states.
7. One license plate for tractor and trailer.
8. Gross weight limit of 80,000 pounds uniform from coast to coast.
9. Consideration on tolls, especially in the East.
10. Gas consideration for gas-burning trucks.

Denver shutdown, December, 1973

I could tell you things that would make you want to cry. Just so you know that when we are revolting—and granted there's nothing more revolting than a bunch of truck drivers—anyhow, we're revolting for a lot of things. This fuel thing is the straw that broke the camel's back. We've stood all we can stand. We can't stand no more.

He's gotta a lotta miles behind him and he's ready for that retirement, but he's got the guts to say, "You want me to shut down, I'll shut down." There's a goddamn brave man as far as I'm concerned. He's gonna take this *Petroleum Buyer's Guide* down to Washington and present it before the committee, or whoever we meet. Some of the things that are in there will make your blood run cold. I won't go into it now because I don't want anyone storming Washington until we're ready for it. I talked to Big Red and the Blue Angel and we're gonna do it. I didn't want it to come to this, but it had to happen.

There are men here from outa town and I sympathize with you, I really do. I'd hate like hell to get caught a long way from home in a situation that's as shaky as this. Believe me, you guys, I sympathize with you. I'm gonna ask you to restrain yourselves, to try and keep the rumors down, to kinda keep from boozin'. War and whisky do not mix. If you see one of your brother truckers strayin' away, say, "Hey, fella. We're all in this together. We're tryin' to do it right." Which is what we are doing.

It's true that in Watkins, a driver has been shot. We didn't receive this report until about an hour and a half ago. One of the local television stations called in 'cause they heard it on the police radio and they were checkin' it out. It is a fact that a driver was shot two miles east of Watkins today. He was wounded in the hand about 3:20 this afternoon. Now I'm not sayin' that somebody laid in ambush to shoot him, or whether it was a stray shot from someone hunting jackrabbits. I don't know where that bullet came from. I hate to think that it was another driver.

There are guys coming down the road now, and we're not twenty-four hours into the shutdown in this area, and there are guys tryin' to get home. They call us at shutdown control and ask if they can go .home. We ask them where they are goin'. Most of them are goin' within six or seven hours from Denver and we tell 'em, "Godspeed. We hope you make it."

I promised you guys that there wouldn't be any brick throwin' and there wouldn't be no shooting, at least not by me or any of my people. You think about this, fellas. You're

Big Cabin, Oklahoma—The independent truckers' protest closed at least three northeastern Oklahoma truck stops Monday and precipitated a tense confrontation between drivers and highway patrolmen when a barricade was erected across U.S. 69 at the Big Cabin exit.

Nearly a dozen highway patrolmen and a half-dozen units from the Craig county sheriff's office were dispatched to Big Cabin to clear the road after one driver parked his rig across U.S. 69 and locked the cab and left.

Several shouting matches then reportedly erupted between the troopers and truckers during the confrontation, but no violence resulted. By evening, Ed Hardy, press secretary to Gov. David Hall, described the situation as "not stable."

—*Oklahoma Standard*

After ignoring the expected pleas and demands, the frantic Ohio Highway Patrol closed the Turnpike from Exit 4 at Maumee to Exit 9 near Cleveland. A number of cars were caught in the jam, and some enterprising truckers tore down a portion of the fence to let them escape. "We have created Turnpike Exit 6½," exclaimed one trucker.

—*Pittsburgh Post Gazette*

drivin' down the road and you're runnin' scared anyhow, because if you don't go you're liable to lose your job and if you do go you're liable to get shot. That's a helluva position to be in. I'd pull over and shut down myself. A lot of guys out here today said, "Can I go home?" I had to tell them that's up to you, but you're here in Denver and you're safe. And the people in Denver care about you.

If there's any kind of a solid backing for any particular issue in truckin', then there's no reason for it to disappear after this happens. Gentlemen, we've got them where it hurts. Let's keep them where it hurts until we're not hurting anymore.

We just have to keep pushin' for what we need. It's life or death now. Last December, there was a shutdown that didn't last too long. There was this unemployed trucker named River Rat who borrowed someone's truck and started running the rig until he ran out of gas. It just so happened that this occurred at a blockade in Ohio. Standing there in his red shirt, levis, and leather vest, River Rat was a prime face for all the television cameras in the area. His face always seemed to pop up on the news. Pretty soon the Coast Guard flew down in helicopters and picked up River Rat and whisked him back to the Department of Transportation in Washington where he was installed in a suite with a lot of telephones. He was told by the people in Washington that the strike was over, and since he was so close to the guys, he should be the first to tell them. He started calling everyone from truck-strike leaders to Governor Shapp of Pennsylvania telling them the strike was over. Nobody could figure out who this guy was that was calling them.

It goes to show that the government understands as little about us as we do about how they run their outfit. And they're in a real quagmire there. With their fees, red tape, bureaucracy, hypocrisy, ICCs, PUCs, DOTs . . . you never know which organization you're working with. They overlap, undercut, and underlap. I mean, the American trucker is drowning slowly, inch by inch, in a bunch of nonsense foisted upon him in the name of good government.

You know what else? These lower speed limits make you awful tired, and it's boring enough driving the Interstates. At least when you were goin' seventy-five you were on your toes 'cause you were looking for Smokey. Get down there to fifty-five and it puts you to sleep. I'd really like to get off the Interstates and drive through some of those winding back roads, through some forests, maybe stop at some small towns. . . .

CITIZEN-BAND RADIO

Come on, good buddy. Come, on good buddy. We've gotta shut 'em down. We've gotta shut 'em down, good buddy. We've got forty minutes to shut 'em down. We're comin' in here following you down. You better shut 'em down. Pull off here at Exit 6 and shut her down. Shut her down or we'll help you shut her down.

Shut her down, good buddy. I'd like to, but the boss says keep on runnin'. You can have this whole damn rig, just gimme the CB radio and the coke.

Shut 'em down or we might just take a match and set that whole thing on fire. No CB radio, no nothing. Just watch that whole thing go up in smoke.

Don't worry about the smoke. You might have to worry about the smoke from my shotgun here.

We'll put a little oil on it and set it all up. Burn that thing to the ground. That's a whole lot of rubber burnin'. We're up to Exit 7 now. You better pull off and shut down. There's a lot of woods along the road up ahead. You better pull her off or we'll help you shut her down. Either way it's gonna be shut down. We'll burn it down around your ears.

Bill Hill, President, Fraternal Association of Steel Haulers, and FASH member

Shotgun blast

I drive a broke-down rig on
"may-pop" tires
Forty foot of overload
A lot of people say I'm crazy
Because I don't know how to take
it slow

I got a broomstick on the throttle
I got her opened up and head
right down
Nonstop down to Dallas
Poppin' them West Coast turn-
arounds

They call me Speedball
Speedball Tucker
Terror of the highways
And all them other truckers
Will tell you that the boy
is mad
To be drivin' a rig like that

You know the rain may blow
The snow may snow
The turnpikes they may freeze
But they don't bother ole Speedball
He goin' any damn way he please

He got a broomstick on the throttle
To keep his throttle foot a-dancin'
round
With a cupful of cold black coffee
And a pocketful of West Coast turn-
arounds

One day I looked into my rear-view
mirror
And a-comin' up from behind
There was a Georgia state policeman
And a hundred dollar fine
Well he looked me in the eye as
he was writin' me up
And said "Driver, you been flyin'"
And "Ninety-five is the route
you were on
It was not the speed limit sign"

In Pennsylvania, truckers formed a blockade at the New Stanton and Monroeville exits of the Pennsylvania Turnpike. Up on I-80 across the entire length of Pennsylvania, CB'ers were active. Command posts were set up at Pocono Truck Plaza, Stop 64 at Lamar, Roadway Truck Stop at Milesburg, and others. The names of the blockade organizers crackled over the air as they directed trucks into blockade positions: Pioneer Cowboy, Big Red, Wisconsin Man, Pistol Pete, Bad News, Daffy Duck, Preacher's Virgin, to name a few.

—from the *Louisville Courier Journal*

CITIZEN-BAND RADIO

Scab, scab, get that eighteen-wheeler off the road or I'll blow your brains out. Scab, scab, shut it down or you'll get a little help. Night's a-comin' on, the night's a-comin' on, you better shut 'em down. You don't even know what work is, scab. You pull into the terminal and have someone else unload, while you go powder your nose and brush your teeth, then jump in a rig and go the other way. You'll get stopped, scab. Sooner or later. Youngstown and Cleveland have shut down. They're on a rampage.

Where's it gonna stop? Round trip from Cleveland to L.A. used to cost $517 for fuel, oil, and tolls. Now it's over a thousand dollars for the same trip. We'll get used to one price and then it will go up another ten cents. Then we'll get more in the hole. It'll jump again and then we'll be wiped out. In ten years there'll be just ten freight companies haulin' every piece of freight in the country. It's now or never.

In all these years, this is the first time I feel like quittin'. All the wives will be happy. All their friends married doctors and lawyers and they got stuck with truck drivers. Damn it, it's a free country. All we are asking for is a little equity. If we can't break out now, then the hell with it. We'll park our trucks in the backyards, turn 'em into jungle gyms, and go on welfare.

"In no instance will we tolerate violence. We can't let a handful of desperados control this thing."
—*Richard Nixon*

I've been driving heavy diesel rigs for 27 years
I've spent my life a-haulin' freight and double-clutchin' gears
Somewhere I've got a family that I never get to see
But I ain't by myself, there's lots of truckers just like me
Now all of a sudden diesel stops are few and far between
Stations closin' down their pumps, what a frightful scene
I'm gettin' kind of worried, what's this country comin' to?

If the world ran out of diesel what would diesel drivers do?
There'd be a lot of trucks for sale, and no one to sell 'em to
We'll all be a-goin' hungry while they raise the revenue
If the world ran out of diesel what would diesel drivers do?

Kentucky—In the Owens-burg area where the strike was scheduled to start early today, drivers promised to stop anything larger than a pick-up truck. . . . One driver, from Gold Hills, N.C., reported that his truck was fired on as he drove along Interstate 84 near Olive Hill. . . .

Last week the drivers were saying that they didn't really want to go to Pennsylvania; now they're saying they don't want to go out at all. Most of those boys have got between $20,000 and $35,000 investment and the rumors they're hearing are enough to keep them off the road. They have to make the decision, since it's their life and their equipment.
—from the *Louisville Courier Journal*

Truckin' Glossary

A-car: short for Autocar, a make of over-the-road tractor. Once known as the "Hercules of Trucks," the Autocar is less frequently seen today because of the rising popularity of the cabover tractor (A-cars are conventional cabs) and because White Motors, which brought out Autocar in 1953, has concentrated on its White Division for its long-haul tractors.
Syn.: Awful-car.

All dolled up: said of a tractor with a customized paint job and accessories, such as chrome trim and pinstripes.
Syn.: decked out, floating chrome, rolling palace, zebra stripes.

All stretched out: said of a truck driven at its top speed.
Syn.: big hole it, build a fire, highball it, clean his clock, dust 'em off, smoke him.

Alligator: an old-time cabover tractor that lacked the tilt-cab mechanism for easy access to the engine. The mechanic had to burrow head-first into the interior of the engine from the driver's compartment. These cabovers were called alligators because they looked as if they were about to swallow the trucker or garageman.

Anchors: the brakes of a truck.
Syn.: Emma Jesse brake, jack-off bar, trolley-valve handle.

Anteater: nickname for the C-model Mack tractor, which is a short-nosed conventional cab; the nose slants obliquely toward the ground.

Aviator: a speeding driver.
Syn.: highballer, leadfoot, cowboy, barrel on down the road.

B-Model: the popular conventional model Mack that is well known by sight.

Balloon freight: light, bulky cargo.
Syn.: load of wind, load of sand, load of suds, feather hauler.

Baloneys: truck tires.
Syn.: rubber, skins, cheater slicks, duals, micks, waffles.

Basket case: an abandoned tractor that has had most of its original equipment stripped off or stolen.

Beaned up: dosed with benzadrine.

    Syn.: bennied, co-pilots, eye trouble, Upjohns, West Coast turnaround.

Bedbug hauler: a trucker who drives a moving van.

    Syn.: relocation consultant, house-number hunter.

Bedsteader: a sleepy driver who cannot be depended on to stay awake on night runs and who is probably in constant search of hundred-mile coffee.

    Syn.: roll and rest.

Believer: a trucker who obeys all rules and regulations of the road.

Between the fence rows: in lane, where a driver tries to keep his truck.

Bible: the ICC's regulations book on trucking, driver, and equipment standards.

    Syn.: brain bag.

Bifocal International: a cabover tractor of limited vintage manufactured by International Harvester in 1960; so named because the cab had two small windows, one on each side, at floor level of the interior. The purpose of the windows was to make it easy for the driver to judge distances between the tractor and other objects or vehicles nearby.

Big rigger: an arrogant trucker, especially one who will drive only the longest and biggest rigs.

    Syn.: sheep herder, tailboard artist, truck jockey.

Blunt-nose: nickname for a cabover tractor.

    Syn.: flat face, flip top, pug, snub nose.

Bob tail: said of a trucker when he drives a tractor without its semitrailer, as in "runs bobtail."

    Syn.: bareback, loose horse, solo.

Bone crusher: a rough-riding truck, usually a cabover because of the location of the steering axle beneath the driver's compartment.

    Syn.: kidney buster.

Boom wagon: a truck carrying explosives.

    Syn.: red label load, suicide jockey, widow-maker.

Boondockin': the truckers' practice of avoiding all major roads and traveling on less frequented ones when running illegally.

    Syn.: back-pasture hauler, moonlight express, wildcatter.

Bubble burner: a rig that runs on propane gas.

    Syn.: juice jockey, percolator, smoker.

Bull hauler: a driver who hauls cattle. Other truckers often refer derogatorily to bull haulers as "hog haulers" because the difference in smell is slight.

    Syn.: grunt and squeal jockey, shoat and goat conductor.

Bumper signs: it is customary among truckers to paint a slogan, name, or nickname on the tractor, usually on the bumper. Most bumper signs fall into one of five categories: 1. the name of the trucker, his wife, his sweetie, his children, or the tractor itself; 2. the name of a song; 3. a colloquial slogan; 4. a humorous description of the driver; 5. a reference to the driver's amatory ability.

The following list is a representative selection of the bumper signs seen on tractors:

Road Runner	Tasmanian Devil
Old Ironsides	Sin or Walk
Thunder Road	Miss Manookie
Home Breaker	Too Little Smoke
Pajama Wagon	John 13:16
Mother's Worry	Ricky Shay
Miss Behavin'	Widow Maker
Big Daddy's Back in Town	Day Late and a Dollar Short
Flying Stud	Jo-Jo Yo-Yo
Chevy Chaser	Dixie Pride
Slo-mo-tion	Blue Angel
Dragon Wagon	Road Fever
New York Belle	Tennessee Walker

Bundle buggy: a delivery truck.
Syn.: candy wagon, city flyer, puddle jumper.

Buy up an orchard: to have an accident and run off the road.
Syn.: belly up, pile up, total it out.

Cabover: a tractor with the engine located below the driver's compartment. The tractor has a straight profile, as opposed to that of a conventional cab, which has a forward projection or nose. The two advantages of cabovers are that they are easier to steer in tight spots or small docking areas and can haul a longer semitrailer and consequently a greater payload.

Cardboard driver: a new driver going through a trial period with a trucking company.

C.B. "Handles" (pseudonyms used by truckers over citizen-band radio channels):

Shadow	Ballbuster
Lead Penny	Dirty Rabbit
Illinois Mustang	Timber Wolf and Polecat
Johnny Yuma and	Rubber Neck
Jeremiah Johnson	Thunder Chicken and
Little Badger	Number One
1077 and 1078	Nosepicker in the
Idaho Diesel	Bugger Diesel
Number One	Little Granny Go-Go
Thunderbolt	Mister Big
Bushwacker and	
Traveling Salesman	

Centipede: a multi-axle tractor-trailer combination.
Syn.: rolling doughnuts, train, Michigan rig.

Cherry picker: an extremely high cabover tractor. Originally the term referred specifically to the old-time cabover model Mack tractor, one of the tallest cabovers ever manufactured.

Choke and puke: a run-down truck stop.
Syn.: heartburn palace.

Christmas tree: a truck with many extra clearance lights.
Syn.: rolling lighthouse.

Clean his clock: to pass another vehicle with great speed.

Clutch artist: a truck driver.

Common carrier: a trucking company that hauls goods for anyone who can pay, as opposed to a contract or a private carrier. Rates and routes for most common carriers are ICC regulated, but common carriers that have irregular routes are not regulated by any government agency.

Concentrator: the trucker of a two-man operation who happens to be behind the wheel at a given moment.

Conventional: a tractor with the engine located in front of the driver's compartment for smoother ride, driver protection, and better vision.

Cut the water off and read her meter: to stop a truck and look for engine or tire trouble.

Dangle the cat: to drive a truck with an engine manufactured by Caterpillar.

Deadhead: to run empty.
  Syn.: hauling postholes.

Death on Truckers: the Department of Transportation.

Dirge: a Dodge tractor.

Divorced: refers to the separation of the members of a two-man operation.

Dog catcher: any rig fast enough to catch up to and pass a Greyhound bus.

Dog house: the covering over the engine in the center of the driver's compartment of a cabover.
  Syn.: dog box.

Double-clutchin' boots: truckers' boots.

Drop it on the nose: to accidentally pull a tractor away from a parked semitrailer without first lowering the landing gear of the trailer to support the front end.

Dusting: driving with one wheel off the side of the pavement and throwing up a cloud of dust; done purposely by a trucker to discourage a tailgating motorist or traffic cop.

Eighteen-wheeler: a five-axle combination that has eighteen wheels in all, or the common large truck.

Emeryville: the cabover tractor manufactured by International Harvester in its Emeryville, California, factory.
  Syn.: corn binder.

Fairyland: any roadside park.

Fifth wheel: the coupling device located on the tractor's rear frame, used to join the front end of the trailer to the tractor. It acts as a pivot point when the rig makes a turn. It also contributes to the "jackknife potential" of winter driving.

Fifty mission cap: a trucker's hat, which usually has several safety badges fastened to it.
  Syn.: gearshift cap.

Fix or Repair Daily: a Ford tractor, considered to be the bane of the driver's existence, to the continued monetary success of the mechanic.

Follow the bulldog: to drive a Mack tractor, whose trademark is a bulldog.

156

Forty acres: the amount of space needed to turn a rig around.

Freightliner: short for White Freightliner, one of the better makes of tractors.
>*Syn.:* fruitliner.

Gandy dancer: a weaving truck.

Garbage Hauler: a trucker who hauls vegetables or fruit.

Georgia overdrive: the neutral gear position, used when a driver, going downhill, throws the tractor out of gear and allows it to coast.
>*Syn.:* Jewish overdrive, Mexican overdrive, midnight overdrive, thirteenth gear.

Give him the wind: to signal to an oncoming trucker that the road ahead is clear and that he can safely speed up without fear of running into radar units or heavy traffic. Different hand signals are used to warn truckers of the various possibilities up ahead.

Goin' home hole: the highest gear or combination of gears in a truck's transmission, in honor of the zealous haste trucker's make when heading home.

Grunt and squeal jockey: a trucker who hauls bulls or hogs.
>*Syn.:* Shoat and goat conductor, Pork Chop Express, cackle crate.

Gypsy: a trucker who will haul any load anywhere for anyone; owner-operator.
>*Syn.:* gippo, moonlighter, wildcatter.

Haul the mail: to speed up for lost time.

Hoo-hooer: a driver who uses the air horn to excess.

Hundred-mile coffee: coffee strong enough to keep a driver alert for at least 100 miles.

I-Can-Catch: Interstate Commerce Commission.

I-men: investigators from the Interstate Commerce Commission.

In Hock Constantly: International Harvester Company.

Jackknife: place the trailer at a sharp angle to the tractor. If a truck jackknifes in an accident, the trailer skids around and hits the tractor.

Jimmy: a tractor manufactured by the General Motors Corporation.
>*Syn.:* Garage Man's Companion, General Mess of Crap, screamin' Lena, Hillbilly special.

KW: short for Kenworth, a make of tractor.
>*Syn.:* katydid, Kay wobbler, Kennie.

Leapin' Lena: a lightweight truck.
>*Syn.:* candy wagon, puddle jumper.

Lie Sheet: a driver's log book.
>*Syn.:* swindle book.

Line driver: an over-the-road, "company" hauler.

Mexican Freightliner: the model-5000 White tractor.

Owner-operator: a trucker who both owns and drives his rig.
>*Syn.:* gypsy, gippo, wildcatter.

Pavement Princess: truck stop hooker.

Pete: short for Peterbilt, one of the most luxurious makes of tractors manufactured and a close competitor with Kenworth tractors in both cost and quality.

Pumpkin: a flat tire.
  Syn.: rider.

Radar Alley: Interstate 90 between Cleveland and the New York State line.

Rags: bad tires.

Rat race: four or five trucks running down the road in a group.
  Syn.: Family reunion.

Reefer: a refrigerated trailer.

Religious road: a broken-up highway with many potholes.

Religious states: states that do not clear snow from their highways: "God put the snow there; let Him take it away."

Ride shotgun: to ride in the passenger seat of the tractor.

Road Aspirin: bennies.

Running hot: running a rig illegally (overweight, out of log book time, or without permits or authority).

Saddle: the driver's seat.

Sears-Roebuck license: the license said to be held by an inferior driver.

Shanty shaker: a trucker who hauls mobile homes.

Shut 'er down: to turn off the ignition.

Sidewinder: nickname for the U-model Mack tractor, a conventional cab with the driver's compartment set off-center to the left.

Sleeper: the bunk compartment behind the driver's seat in any tractor.
  Syn.: slumber slot, pajama wagon, suicide box.

Smokey: a state trooper.
  Syn.: bubble-gum machine, bird dog, Smokey the Bear, big hat.

Squealer: a device in a tractor that automatically records the mileage, hours driven, speed, and number of stops.

Stove: a heater in a cab.

Tandem: 1. two pairs of duals mounted together on a trailer. 2. a semi trailer with two rear axles. 3. generally speaking, a tractor-trailer.

Tap dancer: a delivery truck driver.

Truck stop commando: a trucker who spends more time outside his truck washing it and shining the chrome than he does inside driving it.

Vulture: a spotter plane that circles over highways on the lookout for lawbreakers.

Weeder geese hauler: an operator who needs a silly answer to the question "What do you haul?" He can reply that he hauls geese to strawberry farmers so that the geese can eat the weeds around the plants.

Working for Standard Oil: said of a trucker who drives a rig that burns fuel in excess.

Trucking Publications

Highway Evangelist
Box 9215
Wyoming, Michigan 49509

Open Road
1015 Florence Street
Fort Worth, Texas 76102

Overdrive
1532 North Cahuenga Boulevard
Hollywood, California 90028

Owner-Operator
Chilton Way
Radnor, Pennsylvania 19089

Trucking Humor
P.O. Box 127
Galena, Kansas 66739

Truckers' Radio Stations

KLAC, Los Angeles, California (announcer Larry Scott): 570

KXWL, Waterloo, Iowa: 1540

WBAP, Fort Worth, Texas (announcer Bill Mac): 820

WWVA, Wheeling, West Virginia
(announcer Buddy Ray): 1170

WWL, New Orleans, Louisiana
(announcer Charlie Douglas): 870